Strawberry Blonde
A Poetry Book

Gabriella Loya

Artwork by Amanda Sept
Edited by Griffin Lamb

Thank you Amanda and Griffin, from the bottom of my heart.

The cover and artwork within Strawberry Blonde is all original work by Amanda. Her friendship with Tristan will forever hold a special place in my heart. It was important to me that their friendship be represented within this book.

When I was thinking of the cover, a certain photograph that Tristan took came to mind immediately, and when I found it, the colors spoke to Amanda and I in powerful ways. She took that and made pure magic. Her work and love for Tristan sinks so deep into these pages.

Griffin did all of the editing and gave me (a bit of a lost writer) some beautifully insightful advice. When he sent me back the manuscript he wrote, "the ideas that I came up with in these comments, flowed out of my attempt to just quietly sit with your poems, and really try to take in the meaning of each line, each stanza." This is exactly how I intended my poems to be read, and when he wrote that, I knew he was the one meant to read over my words. For that, I am so deeply grateful.

2

My sweet friend told me something I'll never forget, "grief is not linear". These poems are not linear, or in any kind of order. The darkest days are tangled within the brighter days.

I will always think of my writing as his parting gift to me. Please read slowly, with all of the sound around you drowned out.

Hold my whole heart gently, and enjoy.

To my deepest love,
Tristan Lloyd Kern

Her pages stained by tears,
torn and tattered.

Words red wine blamed.
Ink and paper.

Heart shattered,

putting the pieces back together.
Page by page.

-

Strawberry Blonde

Bold in his knowledge.
Stood in his faults.

His mind: the trunk, steady & growing.

His heart: the branches of a weeping willow, benevolent to the touch.

Hard working hands,
held my heart so delicate.

The eyes of a humble love.

This grief is starting to mold me.

I wake up gripping your sweater so tight.

My nose shoved in the neckline trying to soak up but savor every drop of your smell.

It is starting to carve, and shape me the way the oceans carve and shape its seashells.

The movement of the waves, crashing over and over again, throwing the shells from the shore back out to sea.

This is what makes them authentic, and raw.
Their own.

This is what the grief and mourning is doing to me.
My tears are controlled by the moon like the tides are.

My tossing in the bed is the waves pulling and throwing me like they do to the shells.

And me, who I am becoming through this is like a sea shell, engraved and marked by the sand and sea.

My own.

Cracked, carved, broken but whole, stained, and forever changed.

Crafted by the earth herself.

Traces of you,
left behind.

My arm reaches, pulling my body forward, feet sinking into
the ground. I finally reach. Traces of you leave me falling,
face first, feet sunk. But my heart made it, leaving the rest of
my body behind.

How much I love you

My own heart thrusts out of its body.

When traces of you
find me.

It's the feeling of:

you pulling me in, whispering "I love you I love you I love
you".

Holding your mighty hands, cupped into mine.

Pushing them into my chest wanting them to reach my warm-
pumping heart, in that moment,

leaving me so weak.

When there were no words.

When there was not enough strength in my arms to hold
you close enough,

that's when I just whispered back I love you I love you

I love you too.

"Come back to me."

The words I whither away into.

Feet up,

in your dads old red
truck, radio singing
softly,

as the wind tangled my hair.

Your hand on my sun-soaked skin.

Faces looking ahead, drenched in august
warmth. With romance on our minds,

you looked over your shoulder
to me, one look into your eyes

had me believing in forever
tomorrows. Forever summers.

A fluttering and fleeting summer that will linger
in my heart the way the first summer's sun
saturates the face, making you forget all the
cold months.

Your love lets me forget all the
cold. What a taste our summer was,
everlasting, but over too fast.

These days,
too painful.

Another month passed,

so fast, the rush of wind pulling my hair.
Day one was not real.

Today it is real.

My heart hides safe,

These mountains, your hands, hold my heart.
I stand at the foothills, looking up.

How tiny: me.

How enormous: you.
Find me there my love.
Find me there.

Dip your hand into grief's
eyes, feel the inside of his
darkest parts,

wrap into his tangled veins until you have knotted
yourself to suffocation inside the grief you call him.

Let the people untangle you,

or sit in a grief where you will find nothing but yourself.

-

reach out.

The pain is deep.

It's rooted in my veins.

Running through my blood stream.
When it reaches my heart,

it pumps dynamite into my body.

There is just enough time for me to put my weapons down
and surrender to the war.

I take off my armor.

Fall to my knees.

With my arms risen to the pain.

In that moment, I let the dynamite take over every vein in
my body.

The pain screams at me to feel it.

This pain & this grief isn't meant to be felt lightly.
So I let it scream at me and explode inside of me.
Pain demands you to surrender.

So just surrender.

What a perfectly devised plan it was that I had.

Looking back.

It's almost amusing to think I ever trusted tomorrow. Or the next week, month, year.

Trusting a plan is like trying to keep your eyes focused on a shooting star.

It lasts for some time. Not enough though.

Then its gone and all your left with is the dark sky.

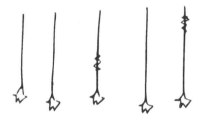

The feeling of missing you is like feeling every beat my heart thumps.

It is feeling every breath that fills my lungs and pushes the air back out desperately.

It is feeling the blood pump through my veins.

It is feeling the scorching hot tears well in my eyes.

It is feeling every bone crack when I stand because it's

just that hard to get up sometimes.

It is feeling the knot in my throat tighten & swell.
It is feeling alive.

Because to really live fully, is to love. And to love, is not easy.

But God, did I love you.

I would rather feel my body's fierce and pulsing pain

every single day, in reminder of how much we let ourselves love, than to feel nothing.

You have shown me something so true, a love that will

fill my lungs, stop my throat, pump in my veins, break my bones, beat my heart, and water out of my eyes.

Nothing feels more real or raw than this.

On your last breath,

the earth sang how in love she was
with you.

Louder than I ever could.

-

Mother Nature

How baffling it is that we may want to go back to that

day. Because then we could say it is day one.

But now we say it is day 61.
Soon it'll be day 161.

Then 365.

The days are passing. They have not asked me if I'm

ready. They just do it.

Life pushes, drags, and pulls us through the days until we
are able to grab it and push and drag and pull our own

way through.

You will always be young.

You will always have smooth soft skin.

You will always have bright strawberry blonde hair.
You will always have your youthful spirit.

You will always be my sweet handsome.

You will always be 21 with only ever life in your eyes.
The devastation and the beauty of it tangle and tousle to
make it something full of wonder.

On day one. Day 161, 365. And on the last day of my own
life,

I will still be in eternal awe of you.

What I would give to jump into your arms.

To have the feeling of your flannel shirt on the side of my face,

as my feet are lifted slightly off the ground

& I inhale your cologne so deeply I could almost taste it. When I close my eyes & think of those moments.

The back of my throat feels like it is closing. My lungs feel wheezy.

I start to feel so heavy that my body could sink completely into the bed but also so light & like nothing that I could float away entirely.

It aches.

I'll never be able to reach far enough to you,

is what is shattering me over & over. Every morning. Every

night.

I fear that I will curl up into fetal position & lock forever.

A sunken ship, slowly descending.

The water is getting heavier. But here I am, surviving it.

Feeling, breathing, yet still sinking.

I let my body go limp, letting these unforgiving feelings pull me down deeper by the limbs.

The way the ocean inhales a sunken ship, I will sink every day over you.

Because you, oh you,

you are relentlessly missed.

Missed as deep as all the oceans' sunken ships. Your absence leaves me feeling lost.

But I am found.

Found not by your mark of the sunken ships ...

But by your earth shattering quake that heaves me back onto shore, evoking me to persevere.

Thank you for not letting me sink.

How exquisite it is, your heaven touched hands pulling us out of our deep dark seas.

Falling into one another as the night starts to descend on us. The lights of the city are dimming.

The wine is dark, cheap.

Warming our throats and tickling our faces. Let the world fight and battle around us.

Because there we lay,

your strawberry blonde curls falling in your face. Your hard worked hands so kissable.

Your
eyes.
Locked
on me.

I think you threw the key to them away forever. Your voice,

Solace and heartened with the gentlest tune. Without a fear or worry in the world.

We loved.

The earth is growling.
I lay silently.

I want to growl with the earth though.
If the earth is mad than so am I.

The earth is crying.
I lay silently.

The branches break through my bedroom window and pull me out of bed.

Throwing me to the tops of the mountains where the heavens met me.

I was reminded that the earth will cry and growl, but the heavens will always sing to me

because you are there.

I wish I could find the words.

I would whisper them in the longing nights.

The words that stream from my eyes past every part kissed by you.

The words that are pounding from my inside to get out. The words that sink my heart at the thought of us.

The words that if you were here, I wouldn't have to speak, because all it took was one look.

And you knew.

May our time away from each other always leave us with no words.

Because it wasn't the words that we gave each other, a gift that I know I'll never find the words to.

They are not earthly words.

For I will not have the words until we meet again.

Have you seen the girl on fire?
How she has loved and lost?

How she has prayed in the winds and heard nothing back?
How she has hiked her highest mountain and never found
heaven?

How she has roared to God with outrage and wrath,

only to feel further astray?

Well this girl on fire,

she has been re-sculpted by the grief.
A girl and her grief.

Some days, it doesn't feel like much either.

But a girl and her grief are a powerful, exquisite mix.

Her world has been flipped, the way her missed one wants
her to see it.

Awakened and abundant with beauty.

She is brutally real, raw, and covets the earth as her most
prized possession.

She is soft as silk with the warmest touch of summers air.
May the girl on fire know that her steps today

will take her to the woman she dreams to be.

And that woman will thank the girl on fire for listening to
every sweet whisper from her guardian angel, with not a
fear.

-

For Sophie

A little lost I feel.

Young but feeling so aged.

Soft smiles in the day fade to weeping breaths in the night. The hours have worn;

the bustle has passed;

the moon has laid a blanket over the city.

My hair let down, my face bare, my skin to your shirt. With nothing but the tender lullaby of our memories singing me to sleep.

A sound so soft,

but at times can have the edges of a knife. Caught in the lullaby, my mind drifts to sleep. Waking the next morning, my heavy legs lift me for another day.

Soft smiles, weeping breaths, lullaby memories.

These are my days.

It is a desperate kind of lonely.
One that I did not see coming.

One that wakes me up in the morning and grabs my heart from all angles.

Pulling and stretching until the very last minute before it completely bursts.

But that's the thing how badly I would rather it just burst and break.

So that it can be over and done with.
This loneliness.

It isn't something to just be done with.

It will get much worse before it gets better.
Finally, I lay down at night.

My heart weary and tired.

I close my eyes in hopes tomorrow will be the day it just pulls and pulls

and at last,
bursts.

Your beauty is
effervescent and
vivid.

Your touch is so familiar it could soothe any lost
soul. Your love is so gentle, a reminder of all the
good in the world.

Your words were lyrics to a song I can no longer
listen to. May you know the depth of my love for
you,

everlasting and rooted deeper than the eldest tree
of our earth.

May you know the longing I have for
our love. For your beauty.

For the beauty our love brought.

It is these hours that I really grasp,

the rawest kind of grief.

I dream in blue.
I cry in blue.

Each falling tear, reminding me—

of the color of the sky that was perfectly painted for us to gaze up to,

the color of the river that we floated down on summers gentle August days,

the color that coats the tops of the mountains we would drive to,

the color of your jacket—

that blue days linger but no longer found.

I couldn't help it.

The words were fluttering and melting off of me at once. Words I fear but still invite to my lips so dearly.

A familiar sound that felt so strange.

If to a stranger it means you are still here, then I'll speak them every day.

I whisper to my heart that words may ease the ache but will not relinquish the pain.

My heart whispers
hold on as long as
you like. It is okay.

Delicate strings of memories.

Fragile conversations between throbbing hearts.
Wandering minds desperate for anything to hold onto.
A world now filled with many winding roads …
Winding roads, do I dare take them?

May my heart find its way again.

Your name, leaving my lips, will be my meaning,
My direction.

With that, I will find my way.

Always my own love
to keep.

Cupped in the palms of my
hands. A young, a golden
love;

a love never tainted, never
unkind, always gentle and
sincere.

Comfort is found in the days we spent, living like
there was never an end.

How naïvely beautiful.

The love you gave me was for me to hold closely
when a tomorrow was no more.

I hold so tightly,

a firefly in my hand, bright and everlastingly
radiant. May it fly away,

but may it never leave me.

A world outside those four walls no longer existed anymore.

It was just the sparkling sound of the fire you made. The aging hum of the cabin.

The howls of the wind sneaking in.

The tickling sound of a mouse in the dark.

There was nothing but us and those four walls Everything we ever needed.

In the middle of a sleeping forest. Safely and sound we were.

As our words put each other to sleep and our minds

drifted off tangled in one another.

Little did we know.

Our year had just begun, the year of a lifetime.

Daintily touching the absence.

Toes tip towards it with weepy
hearts. To sight, a forever
empty search.

To heart, a find never far to
wander. Petals drop as
seasons pass,

surely not gone, sinking their rich color and beauty
into the earth herself.

Decorating the earth with their angel wings, as a
heavenly wind brushes past our desperate eyes into
our ears and touches the most broken parts of us.

This hope hesitant,

this acceptance
reluctant, this
heart weary:

but in the moments of astray, you find me. With the
ease of never needing to look.

-

The Words

Reaching for your sweater.

A piece that laid on you so handsomely.
Residing in the corners of my sheets.

The lingering trace of your smell tempts me.
The dawn light, cold and blue.

Rushing and seeping through the blinds.
The chilling February air,

with fleeting hints of campfire,
maybe wishful thinking.

The rough knit scratching my face, your cologne so faint
but filling my lungs so deeply.

Just for a moment, with my eyes clenching shut.

I'm with you again and it seems a dream to me that a day
hasn't passed.

Here I lay.

1:17 am.

Words and heart beats fluttering around the bed.

Like they might just grow wings and take off

out of my room without me.

Wide eyed awake.

I can feel you reach into my chest. To my heart.

You are planting roses and rivers in it.

Listening to every uneasy beat.

But in the first hours of the new day,

depth filled beauty crafted from your hands,

into my heart. My love,

you plant the roses, for protection;

you plant the rivers, for a wild wonder.

I can fall asleep now.

Knowing you are taking care of me,

stirring my broken heart to rise.

My room filled with the new day's light.
My heart pounding fast,
racing to get back to you.

Wrinkles.

The longest winter.

Lines carved into her face the way waterfalls rush down earths sides.

She smiles when she thinks of you.
Eye bags sinking.

She rises in the morning forgetting and then remembering.
The face of grief is not pleasant, but it is beauty.

Her face is flooded in the nights,
a natural disaster.

My muse

forever painted on my wrist,

the thoughts that spill from my hands to
paper— a bear in his forest

at once lost to us

but no, he's never
lost— pointed by the
heavenly stars.

You look back
to me I send a
kiss goodbye.

May you meet
me soon, but
until then

there are bigger plans for you
my bear. Rest dear heart, rest.

When I think back to our memories,
I view them in flashing slides.

Me sitting next to a film slider.
In a dark room.

Watching us on the projection screen.
I let each slide, leaked and vintage,
melt into my eyes.

The color's warm and grainy.

They flash so quick, and the pieces, fleeting moments, are
broken up.

Creating this everlasting and romantic collage of images.
There is no music, just the clicking of the projector.

There is nothing in the room but the color from each

image painting my skin.

How easy it is to get lost in this, and in the unravelling
film. I want to pause the images and stare at them

forever.

The roll is unravelling so fast; I can't seem to pause
it. These photos, moments, memories.

They are not meant to be paused.
They are fragile, blissful, and delicate.

So here I am, letting each slide flash before me.
Because there is nothing more I want than to watch our
sweet short film.

On repeat.

To go forward as the girl you fell in love with,

I will need the strength from the tallest
mountains. The way the snow covered peaks
reach to heaven... is how my hands must
reach to the Lord;

the way the snow sheds down the
mountain, is how I must let my tears
fall;

The way it lays,
planted and
steady,
boundless on
its earth.

The way the mountain lets the earth carve and cut its
peaks,

For the rooted trees that spread over its hills,

are the parts of you forever rooted in me.

In the sky
a rainbow

caught my eye.

On top of the waves
keeping up with our boat. It
caught my soul.

Resting on the café
door; her hand holds it,
you caught my heart.

Reflecting on my chest

catching each quiet tear like falling stars.

May I find my rainbow when weary,

just like we danced that night in the forest together those
days ago.

May I dance in forests with my rainbow catching each

spin & fall:

painting small moments with your presence.

The way my first breath taken without you here,

left my lungs and got lost in the chilling air around me.

The oceans split and flooded the forests floor.

My skin like the bark on a tree,

shedding away the skin you touched.

We cried with the forest.

"Mountains or ocean?"

He would say mountains before I could even get the

breath to speak.

I would say ocean.

But only an ocean where I can see the mountains.
And he would say only mountains where I can see the
ocean.

Now I say mountains,

faster than my heart will beat.
He gets both now.

What a view it must be from heaven, love.
Me, I'll find my way to the mountains.

Any moment I get.

Because when I am on a mountain, I feel closer to heaven
than ever before.

And him,

I know he will meet me there.

It must be a short visit from heaven to the mountain tops.

When I talk of you

my hands clutch each
other, moving to the
center of my chest
because he is the center of
me, the core of me,

my heart and soul,

the very best part
of me; even in
heaven

he is still changing me; he is forever changing me.

Have courage my dear heart.

You are meant to beat so fast and so loud that I can hear you.

And it will remind me that you are alive, you are pumping blood;

I am alive.

You run deep in my
heart. You run deep
in my veins.

You run deep in my mind, tender
memories. You run deep in my spirit.

You run deep in my skin, the way you t
ouched it. You run deep in my eyes.

They are no longer here to feel the ocean's waves.

They are no longer here to feel the winter's snow on their face.

They are no longer here to feel the earth between their

toes. But now they are the ocean wave that crash into

you,

the soft snow that kiss your nose,
the earth that rests between our toes.

They who have past, whistle through the winds,

flow within the currents, and drum through the mountains.
Just listen.

Heaven is where you are;
earth is where I am, and

in every view that takes my
breath;

I see you.

The hours fly by like minutes.

My body moves in an ache filled motion to my other side. I don't dare open my eyes to the reality of the morning.

But I do.

Being squeezed around the waist. Being spun in circles.

Being lifted by a hug.

Being kissed after being missed.

Being held in the middle of the rushing river on a hot summer day.

Being able to rest my head on his shoulder down an open highway.

All these
memories. They
flash and rush
in.

I feel this feeling—

of the warm sunshine leaking on your cheek. Its fleeting & comforting.

Something you want to last longer, but you know it won't. This is what makes these mornings so hard, but something to treasure.

That night.

There was no sleep, there was no rest.
My heart was choking,

my body was petrified,

and my soul was weakening.
So I closed my eyes.

That is when I knew.
You were safe.

His hands were holding you so gently, so peacefully.
You were untouched by the rocks.

For just half of a second.
My heart could breath,
my body fell into itself,
and my soul trusted.

That is when I knew,

you were no longer with me.

You were safe,

resting with Him.

I so badly want to take
a trip. A trip to our
mountains.

A trip to our
cabin. A trip
to our forest.

A trip to our little fire.

A trip to our own little world.

It was a world I shared with only you.

It was a world that I want back so
badly. It's a world I hope I can
visit again.

A world I can feel you pulling me to, telling me I
can still visit it.

Because you will be
there. Waiting.

It was just once,

but I felt like the moment could last forever.

When I saw you flying down the hill with the ocean in your eyes,

looking back at me with the brightest smile.

It was like you were an angel in heaven, riding to the Kingdom.

So graceful.
So peaceful.
So fearless.
So pure.

Electrified.

When I see it in my head, I see it so clearly, as clear as the rays of the sun flashing onto your face as they beamed through the trees.

I replay that moment in my head over and over and over.

Because it is how I think you found your way to heaven: gracefully, peacefully, fearlessly, purely, electrified.

My sweet friend.

She told me this morning. "God does not waste pain."

I thought to myself ... pain bites pain tears pain rips pain breaks pain stabs pain burns.

The pain can be all at once, short but forever scarring.

The pain can be chronic, long lasting and not letting you forget it for even a second.

God knows this. He knows.

This pain is not going to waste.

Every bite, tear, rip, break, stab, burn...

God is going to use every bit of that, and your heart your soul your mind and your body

will come out more gentle, kind, and soft. Being soft is not being weak.

It's the delicate work of God transcending the pain and darkness

into someone with a past, with a story, with something to share.

Yes, with far too many scars.

But those scars are reminders of the work God and you have done together.

Don't let the pain damage you forever; take the time you need to feel it and let it bite and scratch you.

But when you are ready.

God is there, patiently waiting to work on this with you.

He wants to sew and stitch the wounds.

The wounds will never heal completely, but with God and your soft heart,

you can help heal others,

your guardian Angels thank and honor you for that.

The memories feel
touchable. They feel
close.

The memories feel out of
reach. Distant.

All at the same time.

And I stand at the bottom of a
mountain. Waiting to feel you.

Nothing.

Then I remember.

You are all around me, every breath
I take. Always touchable yet out of
reach.

Because when I touch the trees, I
touch you; and when I breath the air,
I breath you;

and when I gaze upon the setting sun, I
see you. These memories all mine to
remember;

but this earth, you for all to feel.

To love and adore you.

What a privilege it is to be loved and adored by you.

It is not
tangible
nor
visible.

It is the sinking of my heart to my toes.

The slow shut of my eyes for just a
moment. And then there,

I'm sharing the air around me with you again,

my eyes don't dare open because they know what
they will see.

Nothing.

But my heart
knows. It is not
nothing there,

It is you my sweetheart.

The gentle breath of hello I do not hear but feel on
the side of my face.

The tender I miss you, not a sound, just a rush
through the empty chambers of my heart,

finally
filling
with
you.

Don't be sad that I'm crying, I whisper ...

Surrounded by sounds.
Friends laugh,

cheers-ing glasses,
city's bustle,

all a song to my soul.

But its notes do not drown out the sound of this loss. My
most dear song:

his voice.
Please,

stop laughing, I want to say,
stop cheers-ing,

stop the bustle;

everyone stop and be still, so I can listen for my song.
I cannot hear it, everything is too loud.

Time away in my quiet, in my sacred grief, alone
is the only place where I find my song,

his voice.

Standing in the
nights cold,
forgetting to shiver
because

every bone in my body was
warmed. Eyes locked on the
full moon,

The luster and mystique making it so hard to look
away. Even when my eyes fall out of focus, they
find the stars.

He is the moon & the stars.

Our last earthly moment.
Fleeting before our eyes,

Neither of us holding it too tightly because
our belief in tomorrow was euphoric.

Words have yet to be written to describe this feeling.
Our love story ending but tied together in a flickering
moment in time.

Falling into you was like falling off the side of the earth
into the vast universe with my arms spread out,

as if I had wings.

The memory forever grained into my being.

Loudly in the quiet.

She grieves.

Laying heavy on my body,

warming me all the way to my heart,

longing for you to wrap me in it the way you
once did. Your denim, a summer's blue;

your denim, an ocean's blue;

your denim, a winter's mountain
top blue; your denim, my blue.

My blue boy.

Your denim, a piece of you.

My blue boy, the blue morning light chilling
my face. My blue boy, the blue sky where I
search for you.

My blue boy, the color of my sadness.

My blue boy, most
of all the color of
all my joy. The
color of my best
days. The color of
my desire.

The color of the best of me.

Now I wear my blue boy's
denim, as I long for you.

And our blue.

Lonely here without you,

my heavenly days are now with you
in the sky so high.

I reach but cannot touch.
You meet me halfway—

reminding me that heaven is not too far
lonely here without you,

I pictured you
there.

The rest of
our lives.

I pictured you
there.

The winter cold is unfamiliar for the first time.
Spring, warming yet bitter.

Summer, yet to show.
The seasons will change.

The winds will speed and slow.
No matter where I go,

there won't be another you

Dizzy
night,
starry
eyes

dancing under the
moon. Finally, I
thought to myself… I
found you.

The quiet
breath heavy.

though at least I can breathe, everywhere
my tears pain, my face the canvas, my cries
the music

filling a room once filled by you
now only filled by me.

Relinquish the sadness,
it is art.

Art once painted by us and by the love we made;

art now painted by the absence of you pouring out of me.

What pretty tears,
what a soft canvas,

may I hold you while your soul sings her cries?

In solitude is where you meet me, making all that is ugly
a radiant expression of living a life, touched by you.

Your touch honey. My skin silk.

Air humid.

Eyes fogged.

Cherry wine warming us inside out.

Bodies tangled tasting like sea salt.

Your face pressed to the side of mine.

The quietest whispers of love into my ear.

Evergreens paint a green blur to my right.

The ocean ahead, so blue I thought the sky had fallen.
You, my love surely you knew, all I wanted was you.
An island, only hours to stay, fireworks exploded in our
eyes.

Your face lighting up with color.

A heat in our hearts like a forest fire.
Stumbles back to the cabin,

Your warm body silhouetting mine,

as the moon sunk its light into our skin,
and my heart slept soundly next to yours.

The air is warm,
and light. But thick
with ache.

Quiet, the kind of quiet

that your voice can
sink into. No longer a
noise or a sound.

But now an essence that fills my
space. Your voice, a feeling

I find in the silence of a
moment. Time slows
down.

My lungs fill with chilled air off of the
mountain tops. Whispers in the winds.

You meet me halfway.

Our finger tips about to touch barley just before
the noise returns and fills my world again.

Until next time, I'll be listening.

Her two great loves.

The man who danced her around the living room,
her little feet tangled & tripping,

dizzy from him spinning her in the air.

His harmonica filled her tiny ears, singing in her mind.

17 years later

A man dancing her in the ballroom,
her feet tangled and tripping again,
dizzy from him spinning her.

That night, she could hear the harmonica her dad once

sang to her—

how the world changed that night,
how tender her heart felt,

how tender it feels even now.

Nature swept up her two greatest loves,
too good for this earth they were.

May they meet over me;
and with patience,

may we all dance together again.

Neck arched.

Head falling back, so heavy I'm afraid my neck

might give out.

Eyes rolling into the stars,

flooded by salty water that I refuse to

let fall down my face.

Voices of my loved ones around, except yours.

The only one I care to hear right now.

Bitterness wants to roll off my tongue,

but does not make it aloud.

Finally, my eyes focus on a star,

just you and me.

A familiar sparkle in the sky, I once saw in your eye.

Voices once drowned out return in full volume.

And the salty water,

I let it fall down my face.

whispering my bitterness as I arch my head up,

and wrap myself as tight as I can in your denim jacket ...
Transfixed by the sparkle in your eye

I now see in the sky.

Like the waves
all at once

I come crashing in, intense and wildly—

pulling the sand out from its ground, pushing it far and
near.

Yet you pull me back out, the way the moon loves the sea:
smoothing the sand, putting it

back in place, grounding it back into the earth
where it belongs.

You the moon, me the sea—
my waves the grief.

Crashing waves some days wanting to mess up all the

sand in its path, dark and dangerous.

Other days a soft blanket of blue, sparkling crystals

floating atop.

Every day though, no matter what sort of waves might
come, you the moon

always brings me back in.

I look to the sky.

I ask the stars.

Beg the moon. Scream to the sun. Weep to the heavens.

Bow to the mountains. Sink in the soil,

There is where I join the roots of the trees.

Tired and quiet.

I look to the sky Limbs spread.

And say, okay.

The summer heat brought our love its greatest peak
in the sand and soil where we planted our feet.

Open skies & rivers dried
you held my face— those
sacred words

spoken from your pink lips.
Had our bones turned to dust,

the winds would have picked us & our love up,
flying us over all the mountains

above each tree

along the wide open coast

and right to the heavenly doors.

That is how I pictured it would happen at least ...

The winds just needed you sooner.

So may our love and you be carried by them:
through my hair

around my open armed body
and for just one moment,
may I breathe it all in again.
Our summer heat.

You are alive,

written in these pages:

from my heart to my hand and to this paper,

and now

in the hands of our people.

I look to the skies that now keep you safe.
As I stand on the earth that took you from us.
The earth that swallowed you up.

How I want to stomp my feet, in hopes to hurt the

earth the way is has hurt me,

tearing the flowers from their roots, the way you were

torn from me

But there is something soft in the air.
My eyes melt into the view.

My knees fall, kissing the earths ground that

fed you all its beauty.

The earth you once immersed your heart in.

The earth that strengthened and sweetened your soul.

No longer can I contain it.

Running to the foot of the mountain,

I fall to my knees—

digging my fingers into the soil and looking up

with a cold terror

at my greatest thief—

weeping why, why, why did you take him from me?

She sinks her streams and rivers into my eyes,

melts her soil into my skin, carves her edges and cliffs

into my spine, sprouts her wildflowers and trees along

my arms and there is where I felt her.

She fell in love with his soul.

His golden lit, deep-loving, wind soaring soul.

He fell, yet she caught him,

and she carried him to her creator.

The day I meet her, I will weep. But something tells me,

it was not her fault. Something tells me to not be angry,

but to just weep.

She will always know I love him.

The sky's colors,
warm sugar fire
painted by god.

Being in love

a part of me died with you;
yet the sun still rise

and set

on our first night apart.

And in each passing day,

I fear to watch it paint the sky.
Because it is just one more view
without you.

But now,

the sky's colors,
warm sugar fire
painted by god

and the boy holding my heart.

The anger is a monster with no hands but paralyzing strength.

The sadness anchors itself to my eyes drowning them into the deepest seas.

But because my heart was loved by you,

the light that once painted our summers together and the fires that warmed our winter together

fills my soul on each
dark day. Such dark
days.

Though I will always search for our light in the sunshine and fires as the seasons pass.

Lingering, longing, wilting in heat over you.
Rays of gold streak my face.

Hints and hues found in the views now touched by you
You put the dandelions in my hair,

my heart in your hands, and
all the oceans flood your eyes
as do mine tonight.

The air

thick with ache.

Quiet, the quiet
your voice can sink
into.

No longer a noise or a sound,

only an essence that fills my
space. Your voice, a feeling

I find in the silence of a
moment. And as time
slows down,

my lungs fill with chilled air off of the
mountain tops. Whispers in the winds.

You meet me halfway.

Our finger tips just about to touch barley before
the noise around me returns and fills my world
again

Standing in the
night's cold,
forgetting to shiver
because

every bone in my body was
warmed. Eyes locked on the
moon,

my wonder of it all, making it so hard to look away.

Even when my eyes fell from focus, they somehow
found the stars.

The time I'll never see again

is weighing on this heart of mine.

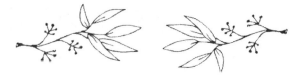

I lie on my side.

A breeze swept my face. My eyes tightened.

I could hear the sounds of the morning:

birds, quiet, cold.

I heard no voices, just the chilling silence:

those mountains casted on me,

the air, the trees,

the silence of your departure.

In my screams there was no sound,

that I might hear the peaceful serenity around me

of that forest that took you.

This anger exploits me.
With each sting, she dies.
Sting after sting after sting.
Only more death.

And this anger scares me.

To love each moment is to hate it as well.
So I love

And I hate
each moment

of this angry summer
without you.

The
humbled
bear, salt of
the earth
her delicate
gift.

Eyes of strength and a
lionhearted soul. Brave in his
steps,

mother nature's most captivating
protector. My humbled bear.

My body felt cold.

But I think I left it for one moment.
Still, laying on my back.

Arms and bare feet hanging limp to my sides.
My dress slipping off of me.

Hair hanging low.

The music and our friends' laughter softly faded into the
distance below me.

Muffled noise covering me like a blanket.

You carried me into the sky,
Dark and quiet to most.

You showed me the stars that night.

You danced them up my body and poured them into my
eyes,

spinning me around so dizzy that the stars

melted together, drenched in their light.

My eyes wide,

you carried me back down,
back into my body.

Where it was still cold.

But I see you now,
there with the stars.

It is sick. My heart, my liver, my lungs, my blood,

black and imploded, with this sickness.

My tears ignite my face into searing flames.

This anger has turned to sickness today.

I can feel it creeping through my veins,

yanking out the lump from the center of my throat for everyone to see.

The table in front of me drenched with my insides,

potent and leaving me hollow.

All this time that we have been apart,

is pulling my own body apart.

Piece by piece, limb by limb,

heart and soul.

Until only bones are left sitting in this chair today.

The earth feels wounded without you.
It must hurt like me.

But the air is warm.
The air is still.

The sky reflecting its pale blue into the ocean.
It sparkles.

The light, strawberry blonde
golden

away from the city,

in a place where I can hear her hum.

The air around me
once your breath—
warm, still, and steady.

The ocean's sparkle I once saw in your eyes.

And that strawberry sun, I once ran my fingers through it
As I look out in front of me, nothing can be wounded.

She has you painting the skies with her.

I fell in love with an artist, who has not lost his
brush but now helps paint

the skies and seas and mountains.

For us to
know
you are
not far.

Your art, my love,

has brought me to my knees, flooded my eyes, and
changed my world.

I haven't let go of the kite.
It soars around me,

Above me.
In me.

Through me.

I delicately string it through my fingers.
Not mine to hold, it never was,

The heavens will let the kite fly so much higher.
Only can fly so high while clutched in my hands.
Letting go, feels so far, out of sight.

But thinking of all the skies the wind will take it to,
my fingers release.

One by one.

And as I watch it fly,
I feel myself fall.

And magic.

Aging over you is perplexing and something I am not ready for.

But time will never ask me if I'm ready.

I fall to my knees with my arms raised high,

my body left with a gaping wound.

My eyes cast to the daunting sky,

where through the haze,

I see our love shooting past the night,

still alive, still golden.

May I find you again one day,

and thank you with every last kiss in my being.

I reach into myself.

Finding nothing more,

but these words,

these pages,

and a life left to live for him.

We made it through.

These pages have been the first 365 days without him. A year that has carved my heart into something I never thought to be. To have this book be in the hands of mine and Tristan's loved ones, well, I welcome the days to come with a little more warmth because of that. With all of my heart, thank you for reading my words. Writing this poetry has saved me. I can only hope that I am able to give you something to help speak on the grief and heartache of your own.

As we step forth on this earth feeling all of the love lost, may we always know that it has not gone far.

My love to you,

Gaby

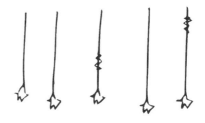

96669021R00061